SELECTED POEMS BY
H. C. ten Berge

FOREST
BOOKS
London & Boston

Edited by Theo Hermans
Translated by Theo Hermans, Greta Kilburn,
Yann Lovelock and Paul Vincent

PUBLISHED BY
FOREST BOOKS

20 Forest View, Chingford, London E4 7AY, U.K.
61 Lincoln Road, Wayland, MA 01778, U.S.A.

FIRST PUBLISHED 1991

Typeset in Great Britain by Cover to Cover, Cambridge
Printed in Great Britain by BPCC Wheatons Ltd, Exeter

All rights reserved. No part of this publication may be
reproduced, stored in a retrieval system, or transmitted,
in any form, or by any means, electronic, mechanical,
photocopying, recording or otherwise, without the
prior permission of the publisher.

Original poems © H.C. ten Berge
Translators' Introduction © The translators
Introduction © Jeremy Reed
Translations © The translators as listed

ISBN: 1 8561 000 49

British Library Cataloguing in Publication Data:
a catalogue record is available
from the British Library

Library of Congress Catalogue Card No.
90–85576

Forest Books gratefully acknowledge the financial support of:
the Commission for the European Communities, the
Foundation for the Production and Translation of Dutch
Literature and the Centre for Low Countries' Studies
(University College, London)

Contents

INTRODUCTION *by Jeremy Reed*   vi

From POLAR SNOW (*Poolsneeuw*, 1964)
    Winter tree *(TH)*   2
    Diary 30/xii *(TH)*   2
    Greenland fossil/an icy poet *(TH)*   3
    Jacob without angel *(TH)*   4

From SWARTKRANS (*Swartkrans*, 1966)
    −88.3°C *(TH)*   6
    Swartkrans *(TH/PV)*   11

From PERSONAE (*Personages*, 1967)
    Monologue in the Vinson Massif *(TH/PV)*   22

From THE WHITE SHAMAN (*De witte sjamaan*, 1973)
    Maker & Model *(TH/YL)*   30
    The White Shaman: An Initiation *(TH/YL)*   32
    The Other Sleep *(TH)*   34
    Second Song of the Shaman *(TH)*   41

From VA-BANQUE (*Va-banque*, 1977)
    Tongue Tied *(TH)*   46
    The Lusitanian Variant *(TH/PV)*   50

From NEW POEMS (*Nieuwe gedichten*, 1981)
    The Hartlaub Gull *(GK)*   62
    Intra Muros *(TH/YL)*   65

From TEXAN ELEGIES (*Texaanse elegieën*, 1983)
    A Semblance of Reality *(TH)*   72

From SONGS OF ANGUISH AND DESPAIR
    (*Liederen van angst en vertwijfeling*, 1988)
    Two poems *(TH/YL)*   80

From RITES OF PASSAGE (*Overgangsriten*, 1992)
    River Landscape with Blue Bottle *(TH/YL)*   84

Translators: *TH:* Theo Hermans
               GK: Greta Kilburn
               YL: Yann Lovelock
               PV: Paul Vincent
All punctuation and capitalization follows the Dutch original.

H.C. ten Berge

About H.C. ten Berge

Although he is known primarily as a poet, H.C. ten Berge has also published prose fiction, essays, and translations. His early poetry was marked by a bare, concise diction, a language full of discontinuities and pared down to essentials, so as to evoke powerful sentiments while avoiding sentimentality. The later work is more fluent and melodious, more overtly personal, intent on combining innovative and traditional elements, lyrical and intellectual impulses. The poems, usually grouped into cycles in which different voices and viewpoints combine to form multi-layered narrative sequences, range widely in scope and theme, and incorporate a variety of historical and literary references.

The openness to the outside world which marks Ten Berge's poetry is apparent also in his numerous translations. Apart from renderings into Dutch of some of Ezra Pound's *Cantos* (1970) and of contemporary fellow poets – Kenneth White, Christopher Middleton, Mark Strand, Xavier Villaurrutia and Gunnar Ekelöf among them – they include texts well outside the Western tradition, from Japanese Noh plays to Aztec sacral and secular hymns. His translations in the ethnological field culminated in a three-volume annotated collection of myths and fables of North American Indian, Inuit (Eskimo) and Siberian peoples (1974–79).

Ten Berge's prose fiction shows the hand of the poet in its meticulous wording, visual imagery and imaginative power. His protagonists are typically emigrés, travellers with an uncertain destination, rootless individuals who have at best a tenuous grip on reality and on themselves. Among his major works in prose are the travelogue 'The Bears of Churchill' (1978), the novellas 'Frosted Glass' (1982) and 'Self-Portrait with a White Woollen Hat' (1985), and the novel 'The Secret of a Cheerful Mood' (1986).

Born in Alkmaar (Netherlands) on 24 December 1938, H.C. ten Berge now lives in Zutphen as a full-time writer. He has travelled extensively and spent longer periods in Central Europe and in North and Central America (Greenland, Canada, Texas, Mexico).

Introduction

In every age there exist two forms of poetry. The popular, which is predominantly concerned with commonplace issues, unrefined and untested by the imagination, and the continuous, by which I mean a poetry which owes its origins to archetypal or psychic premises, and shapes its vision of the present by universal rather than social tensions, and is therefore the more likely to be of value to the future.

The poetry of H.C. ten Berge belongs to the latter category. Complex, hermetic, shamanistic by virtue of its access to myths and primitivism, richly textured in the montage effect it achieves by juxtaposing past and present, Ten Berge's poetry is nevertheless accessible and vitally alive to the preoccupations of the age in which we live.

In this generous selection of his work, which draws on three decades of writing, beginning with *Poolsneeuw* (Polar Snow, 1964) and traces his poetic journey right up to the present day, we meet with an internationalist writer, and one who is uncompromising in his individual search for truth. There is an anarchic, subversive undertone to some of Ten Berge's poetry, particularly when it opposes the acquisitive greed of material capitalism, which goes hand in hand with the poet's celebration of whatever vivifies the earth, whatever is built out of the correspondence between the word and the poet's measure of it as inspiration.

Something of the isolation, the price paid by the contemporary poet who refuses to sell out to the media, is expressed in Ten Berge's 'Ill-adjusted sonnet' from *Nieuwe gedichten* (New Poems, 1981).

> *Even as I read*
> *how this country's underworld of hacks*
> *keeps on its feet*
> *with frenetic trifles,*
> *poetry hides as it always does*
> *in abandoned rooms, in your bare cell*

Introduction

twilight and water as far as the winter-dyke
a girl comes by on a white horse

Poetry in Ten Berge's terms remains underground—'poetry hides as it always does/in abandoned rooms, in your bare cell.' It has nothing to do with hacks, abusers of the word, falsifiers of the poetic vocation. And that girl who enters the picture on a white horse takes us somewhere else, into a visionary landscape. It is the verbal becoming the visual, the poem entering a fluid dimension.

English poetry from the fifties onwards is a history of limitations. There is observation without risk: superficial acceptance without commitment. Rejecting the imaginative infusion of surrealism, English poetry has stolidly ensconced itself in the world of social commentary. Its European counterpart has pursued an independent orbit, maintaining a trajectory which embraces experiment with subjective findings, realism with the open-ended narrative of the unconscious.

Ten Berge's work belongs to a school of expression which, beginning with the Olsonian Black Mountain School of poetics in the sixties, began to make the self-conscious art of writing into a subject for poetry itself. What happens prior to words meeting the page is a dramatic arena in which the imagination works to assert control.

The mouth opens like a golden box,
the tongue swims around, emitting words
at intervals

love and poetry
are forever on the tip of one's tongue

what began as a chemical reaction
between brain and bum
finds its shape
when pushed into expression

Here the psychophysical unity that provides for the writing of poetry is seen to have magical origins. The mouth is of

Introduction

course a golden box: words representing levity, graceful notes by which the line dances in accordance to inner rhythm. And Ten Berge's poetry is very much about how the world is transformed by language: 'By poetry I can stand a stone in the sky or earth a cloud, so that it sits outside my window like a grounded messenger.'

At the heart of Ten Berge's poetry is his identification with the myths of Northern peoples, about which he has written substantially in prose, and the blinding, white snow world which forms the backdrop to his poetic landscape is one in which men resist technological encroachment. Ten Berge identifies with a mode of expression, a reading of the universe which material ideologies have tried either to ridicule or suppress. What the rationalist thinker would of course designate as insanity is, in terms of poetry, the highest form of imaginative expression. But people and poets are persecuted, and Ten Berge portrays this well in 'Diary 30/xii'

> *I carry wood in a world that is braced for me.*
> *while right in the head I was a deserving image-carver,*
> *but since the cold set in my fingers have grown stiff, the whet-*
> *stone is cracked and the chimney-jack gives no*
> *sign of life.*
> *I got snowed in. and work is piling up, waiting*
> *for the shrike of the wintry word to rise in*
> *the sun.*

It seems to me that a poetry divested of the potential to create the marvellous, is a poetry of negative sensibility. Images should attain that transformative level whereby anything may happen and does. Octavio Paz reminds us that 'Poetry either leaps into the unknown or it is nothing.'

Ten Berge's voice is insistent, powerfully individualized and demands attention. He reaffirms the poetic calling as a solitary, intrepid elucidation of the universe by the individual. Poets who seek refuge in the collective, and look for reassurances of their criteria by the validation of it in others, play no

Introduction

part in this dangerous undertaking. And in subject matter Ten Berge can shift from lacerating Harry Hilton and his chain of hotels – the man who 'drops timely magnetic turds/ Of capital in prefabricated chambers' – to the metempsychosis of the soul as it is understood by the shaman.

to leave the tent on all fours
for a distant rustling of wings

eye to eye with the white wolves
of a brief dawn

The sheer range of these poems, crossing as they do continents situated in time and space, makes them plastic and multivalent, touching the corners of the world and then feeling for new possibilities.

In introducing H.C. ten Berge to English readers, I feel privileged to have become acquainted with his poetry. One lives for the excitement of discovering a new poetic voice, an addition to that chain in which, Eluard says, 'The doe between leaps likes to look at me.'

Jeremy Reed
1991

About the Translators

Theo Hermans is Reader in Dutch at University College London; he has published scholarly work on Dutch and comparative literature and on Translation Studies and has translated poetry into both Dutch and English. Yann Lovelock is the author of several collections of original poetry and prose; he has translated from Dutch and French and written a study of modern Dutch poetry in English translation. Greta Kilburn is a freelance translator living in Amsterdam. Paul Vincent, a former lecturer in Dutch at London University, now works as a commercial translator in London.

Acknowledgements

The present anthology contains selections from all of H.C. ten Berge's poetry volumes, from *Poolsneeuw* (1964) to the as yet unpublished *Overgangsriten*. As the poems are usually grouped into cycles, these are given here unabridged, with only two exceptions: for reasons of space 'Maker & Model' and 'An Initiation' have been reduced from three and seven poems, respectively, to two.

Thanks are due to Mr Ten Berge for his permission to publish these English versions of his poems. I am grateful also for his encouragement and helpful advice over the years, and for his readiness to give the translators a free hand. I particularly appreciate his kindness in letting me see a typescript of *Overgangsriten*, due out in 1992.

A number of poems in this collection first appeared in the magazines *Adam, Cencrastus, Chicago Review, Comparison, Contemporary Literature in Translation, Dimension, Dutch Crossing, Little Word Machine, PN Review, Prospice, Stand* and *Writing in Holland and Flanders*, and in the volume *Dutch Interior* (ed. J.S. Holmes and W.J. Smith, New York, 1984).

All translations have been thoroughly revised for the present publication. I am especially grateful to Yann Lovelock, not just for the practical assistance he offered but above all for his invaluable help in reworking and vastly improving those earlier renderings. If the verse in this book comes at all close to capturing the poetry and music of the originals, this is entirely his doing.

We are grateful to the following publishers for permission to reproduce some poems from their collections: Meulenhoff Nederland b.v. (*De witte sjamaan*, 1973, 1986, 1988; *Leideren van angst en vertwijfeling*, 1988; *Overgangsriten*, 1992); De Bezige Bij (*Va-banque*, Amsterdam, 1977; *Nieuwe gedichten*, Amsterdam, 1981); and Athenaeum-Polak & Van Gennep, Amsterdam (*Poolsneeuw*, 1964, *Swartkrans*, 1966, *Personages*, 1967).

(T.H.)

from: *Polar Snow*

Winter tree

As if underground there is poetry
in man / it outgrows the bark
a bird shivers in my hand
the afternoon's sun snows hieroglyphs
about the bole

Diary 30/xii

I carry wood in a world that is braced for me.
while right in the head I was a deserving image-carver,
but since the cold set in my fingers have grown stiff, the
whetstone is cracked and the chimney-jack gives no
sign of life.
I got snowed in. and work is piling up, waiting
for the shrike of the wintry word to rise in
the sun.

Greenland fossil / an icy poet

Sun old wastrel
chasing tail on other planets

cold stalks his flesh
like hoary shingles
needles pierce
the petrified backside of speech

foundations of poetry
lie bared and open;
the eye stares petrified in air

a gaunt view of what still lives
of what dispowers itself

the mouth half open and assailed too early
has just laid the first letter

silence releases no howl

polar snow: a myriad weapons hang glittering
in the sun

Jacob without angel

Córdoba,
Lejana y sola

Motionless I try to catch
your gestures
as I write
the poem like a human being is a conceivable form
I break the agreement

nothing should be said
to reach after
the angel's inconceivable image
though your shadow falls over every word
in every face you conceal yourself superbly

so I sit on view by the roadside
my child is playing round the turn
the donkey nibbles at dust in the sun
will I ever reach the town?

an agreement is made to be kept.

from: *Swartkrans*

–88.3°C

Endurance

Crushed between fields of white
Its ice-coated rigging climbs up,
The guerrilla that feeds on cold mounting
Crazed companions, the glass compass.
Like a cathar in slow-motion suicide
The stern splits and mates with menhirs of the ice-pack.
Clusters of hail riddle the deck

A twelve-bore projects from the wheel-house

 ## Air traffic

Cast shadow spreads like twilight
Behind the sentinel range. the hercules
Hurries across ridges towards the string of bases,
Cirrus streaks gather on wings; late flight
Wrist-high rime is waiting on landing strips
Space solidifies in darkness

Near lion and serpent-bearer spica now crouches
Hips like miss universe

Logbook / –88.3°C

"How I imagine harassing this legal
Regime. in cabins a voice reads
The 3 rules of discipline and the 8 recommendations
The snow-cat crawls ahead of convoys to vostok.
Clefts, numerous as mines surround the field
Detector disks feel electronically for the trap
While around us a swift spy
Skims the chromium-plated horizons"

Prospecting

I drill punctures in the plateau's
White shroud; samples are trapped
In the cylinder head. granitic gneiss whose density
Attests a coldness determined within the hour
As post-silurian, god knows what ice-age.
Leaf fossil: that continues to devour time while I
Squander limits / then spitefully
Destroy its nervature

Aerial

This ear anchored
In cell-restraint and unshadowed
Corrugated roof
Wrapped like an ink-blot in the pure white
Desert film.
Code is germ-white
With language

It transmits messages at the hours claimed. time
Kneads hatred and bares contacts under its hood

Antarctic convergence

World without smell of bread and ashes or
Rot, where moss and algae convulsed
People the cliffed coast and man doubts his skin
In the gruff archive of the planet

Latitude where the curtain of rabies grazes
The seas, the rugged canker of ice encircles the ship
Like a rebel who smiles in perfect ambushes,
Fumbling with his mauser

Nobody

I lie in belts of absence; my shoes
Pinch at the edges where a field of steel
Points composes the black winter coast.
I leave no impression and watch the glacier roof
Calving in cool amniotic fluid

The wind sometimes floats a white spider to my face

So saying, he disappeared among the shades of the pine-
Tree at akasaka, and night fell

Night glass

Blind as bats they climb from the hatches
After months of halfsleep and hate
In which the comic turns wet blanket.
No women pass ice terrace or reactor reserves
Where naked scientists practise karate, a wind-gust
Whirls red snow. I take off the mask;
A light-show sweeps the night behind its crater rims

Slowly the hemisphere is relinquished to infiltrators

Morbus aedificandi

Penguins limping among plastics and the high-priced call-note
Of plastered begums; the biscoe-bank ltd
Opens counters, thinks and drills a blizzard of
Banknotes into the iron restraint of a safe. likewise
Nimble hilton builds his 7 hotels in a fever
(Fragrant cages, mc murdo S.w. cent. heat. by
Nucl. pow.) and drops timely magnetic turds
Of capital in prefabricated chambers

for E. Shackleton and E.T. Tolstikov,
guerrilla fighters of a continent

Swartkrans

Swartkrans

Boring into this manhole
(Each stratum's a death sentence ago)
I split silicates. jagged-edged dustcloud:
Shaft in mirror-image above the workings

While redneck gives chase till knives
Are buried in the backs of savages
Other dead encounter downward forces:
Cones slowly penetrate the earth

The airforce soars above
But all I can do
Is grub for a word, a progenitor
Who's a dead loss

My nerves throb in molars
Tongue gradually denies premature speech
Sediments have shifted
Time displaces my jawbone.
Where australopithecus feels his cranial ridge
I have a clear view, but that's all

Brassempouy

When preachers weren't yet dictating death
Or profiteers proscribing hard-up tyrants
She was found among dodder and broom-
Rape

There were those who spoke dismissively of her
Although her ochre neck in no way belied
The severity of the body.
True, her breasts did not stand up to stylization
Her womb seemed scarcely receptive to any
Movements but those that precede littering

She nonetheless deluded scholars:
She was origin, and also: primordial. years
Mounted to millenia
She was probed, they took her
Measurements and had her finally kaltgestellt as heretical.
As an object of lust she'd scarcely awakened desire

(Others believe: she was randy as a spider, see
Also lespugue, recorded shortly before
Brassempouy. an immediate sensation, tossed
And turned from hand to hand

Silent, mouthless
They bore centuries within them)

Lübeck

Too late for travemünde.
Body, location, time
Are draped heavy as chains.
Words react with each other
The matter is inextricable for it
Entangles me and gnaws

I travel back and had
Moved in with lotti vorstan.
Bag-of-bones with a human face;
Before (tackled in the bushes, put to the
Question and lashed about the neck)
I was nearly done for

I gave her a book of hours
She adjusted her hennin
Then I gave her my dagger
Although it was winter.
And she moved the ring
Of amber on her finger

Belated lover of unproven manhood, my throat
All peppers and acids
Said she: was do bist das was ich
Ich han vil erliten
She smelled her mate in me
Who shipped tobacco past the cyclades

Across centuries I see her humane head
Beside that eroded kisser.
It starts to snow, time
And city got bogged down there,
Wintry. Boils began to
Branch out into creeping tooth-decay

Later it turned out she liked playing underdog
In church doorways. lollard with his lute
I played along for, so to speak
She served gods with her arse.
When I moved on
She'd caught a dose from me

Nemrud Dagh

Truculent as ageing bulls mountains stretch
As far as the western euphrates
Drought hacks and traces roads full of inscriptions.
I hitch a ride from the base and mashallah
What a girl. we get stuck
In commagene where antiochus the anatolian
Embossed a broad terrace with divinities

No camel and no track. the landrover
Won't budge; she muttering unintelligibly
To herself, me humming damnation as if I
Don't see her. ceaseless sunlight burns down,
Concerted gibberish unites.
Too much play in the steering

She points to the terrace where birds
Have petrified: toppled statue
Stares into riven earth

Heads lie patterned with cracks, scattered
Among the boulders,
Glaring mutely at the vehicle

Fissure: the ground starts moving on both sides of the wheels

Earth shifts and draws a net of cupreous
Eyes around us

The staring is cutting into us already.
We're clearly alone

Andes

> White of winter is over her head,
> Is over the husk of her shoulders;
> Her eyes no more like the colour on distant mountains.

the mountain range burns down to its basins,
its belly swollen and wrinkled with hunger.
capac is dead
late daughters
show me totora reed used for building ships

the young huaina who steers me across lake
titicaca; water offers a journey without past.
no dead mine
at potosí,
no silver is paid for in syphilis

> Komachi was in her day a bright flower;
> She had the blue brows of katsura,
> She used no powder at all

capac is dead: from quito to cuzco his daughters
still stand in woollen clothing, markets
a day's journey away
kept ablaze
by the god of light as unplastered ruins

she shows her supple skin with its natural
lettering; lips talk me into time past
the ring never grew
tighter than that: in this white
shirt stands a threadbare image sweating out figures

beside her skin my mass-produced hide is mere preserve
her breasts are encircled needle-sharp untranslatable
by lines which she says the sun drew there.
pyramids
have their structures

⁕   Who are you?

I am the ruins of ono,
The daughter of ono no yoshizane

How sad a ruin is this:

houses like the boxes of the dead, a fist of sleep
leans on midday, boulders stand like tumours
behind the square and are assembled sunlight:
central-massif
in miniature

brief item: since pizarro lost his face
no god has died in wombs
apu illiampu lies grafted in her features
lice lingered by the fun-fair couch
of her birth

She cannot hide it at all,
She goes begging along the road,
She wanders, a poor, daft shadow.

six pm
food is being served

Albi

In the dry grass of tarn slumbers
Robert le bougre:
Evident ancestry of vertebrates
With outrider's marrow; who was covered
By the powers that be and still landed in jail

No, sooner meister konrad who had a muzzle like a mule
Who swiftly heard confessions and crossed
Himself before stroking human backs with whips;
Who blew his reign of terror in particular
Under the shifts of beguines

In the dry grass of tarn
Raimund now swears his umpteenth
Oath. he bites the dust before the whore
Of babel with her biblical manners.
And what says the pope? he infallibly cuts compulsory figures

Exterminare closes every discourse

Dogs scour the grass in pauperized frocks
Farmyards lie empty
Empty too the weavers' cottages
Gutted and bitten. true, the south lies empty
As a sheath, and red
And there domini canes sniff
The breathtaking perfume of their habits

In the dry grass of tarn sleep
The women of albi

'Water and shadow, shadow and water'

I fashion a flowering image
Considering that nicholas is being fed
On time and I read aloud to her from lorca
— Rosa, la de los camborios
Sitting on her doorstep, mourning
With two severed breasts on a platter
And the guardia civil holds the gipsy town
To ransom —
Then I quite like love
If it's love that's meant

And one can sing it all
As indeed they do, overflowing with stammer and talk

True such flowery chatter
Of thighs breasts soon grips one in its vice
(Mind you it's also rather nice)
Feeling like a potter for a while
With hands moulding soft clay
The tender bowl of a breast
The sweet full vase of a thigh

I think of rosa, la de los camborios
And watch how nicholas
Clutches her breast with little twiggy hands.
Then I quite like love

I fashion a flowering image for timorous hearts
Brim-full of violence

Notes:

Swartkrans: a site in the Transvaal (South Africa), where humanoid fossils have been discovered, including cranial and skeletal fragments of Australopithecus. Characteristic of Australopithecus are a relatively light jawbone, indicating an omnivorous rather than a herbivorous creature, and an ape-like cranial ridge leaving room for only a small braincase. 'Redneck' (stanza 2) is a familar nickname for a white South African.

Brassempouy and *Lespugue* (in the Landes and Haute-Garonne, France): sites where prehistoric statuettes have been found, almost certainly representing fertility symbols. The German word 'kaltgestellt' (stanza 3) means 'put on ice, put in cold storage'.

Lübeck combines modern motifs with a 15th-century *danse macabre* as found on the walls of the Church of St Mary in Lübeck. A line like 'was do bist, das was ich' ("I was once what you are now"), here in an apocryphal Low German and attributed to the fictitious character Lotti Vorstan, would often occur in a *danse macabre*, spoken by Death. The words "Ich han vil erliten" ("I have suffered much") are from a Middle High German poem. Medieval prostitutes frequently went about their business ("serving God with one's arse") in church portals, which would have dances of death painted on their walls.

Nemrud Dagh: a mountain in the Commagene region, near the Euphrates river in northeastern Syria. Antiochus I, whose Seleucid kingdom was annexed by the Romans in 69 BC, had an imposing mausoleum built here in around 30 BC. Extensive remains can still be seen today.

Andes combines fragments from Ezra Pound's version of Kiyotsugu's 14th-century Noh play *Sotoba Komachi* (the indented stanzas) with references to the conquest of the Inca empire by Pizarro's band in the 1530s. "Huaina" (stanza 3) is Quechua for "young man". The "capac" mentioned twice is Hayna Capac, the last Inca emperor to rule a united empire; his heart was buried in Quito, the rest of his body in Cuzco. The silver mines at Potosí are southeast of Lake Titicaca. Apu Illiampu is a mountain on the eastern shores of the same lake.

Albi refers to the medieval Cathar stronghold in the Tarn region of southern France. "Meister Konrad" is Konrad von Marburg, appointed Grand Inquisitor by Pope Gregory IX in 1227 and murdered in 1233. Robert le Bougre, made Inquisitor by the same pope in 1233, was a former Cathar minister himself (hence his nickname: "the Bulgar" or "the bugger") who had become a Dominican friar. "Domini canes", Latin for "the Lord's hounds", puns on the name of this order. The Raimund of stanza 3 is Raymond VII, count of Toulouse, who had the Treaty of Meaux forced on him by the French King Louis VIII and Pope Gregory IX in 1229.

"*Water and shadow* . . ." alludes to the "Romance de la Guardia Civil española", the final poem in Federico García Lorca's *Romancero gitano*.

from: *Personae*

Monologue in the Vinson Massif, a commentary

1.

So we freeze in, dead abundance at 13,000 feet
with fossil game and skeletons
and sand, ores, graphite; we're a frozen white turd
in the lime desert of the cap

said
petrus toen
1480:

cvr homo mortalis caPvt ExTRViS aT mOrieries EN vertex
talis sit modo calvvs eris
why mortal man have your portrait painted, for look, you'll
have to throw in your hand sometime and be bald as this skull

poles shift
skuas swarm round the voice
that rare bird man has hatched an egg
here on the rocks, there in the lowland of poplars and
                                           petrochemicals

> The cap cracks, tons of granite from the mountains are crushed in the rifts. Chain reactions of tremors, the andes subside and slowly the continent rears up in its gruesome release. Three hundred, six hundred feet – and still not over – seas churn, the water rises, lands submerge, a continent has ceased to exist, swept away, sunk beneath the masses that surge forward over coasts and sea-defences. People drown clinging to gutters, tree-branches; the president leaves for an unknown destination and never arrives. Eskimos snigger in their paradise where wild plant-growth shoots up like in deserts after rain. Plague germs stir after centuries of sleep. Red death. On the equator it turns cold. Women, children shiver bareskin and wrap themselves in tree-bark, fearfully. They die with

eyes wide-open. Men sweep across frontiers in armies, fighting in neighbouring states for every foot of firm ground which crumbles in their dying grasp. Wall Street collapses, the high-priests come pouring out with flapping jackets, wringing their hands at the mammon plummeting down dow jones. Every compass goes haywire, ships are lost in the interior of brazil, the congo. In cologne a cruiser is caught in the web of spires. Ceylon switches from coffee to onions. At the south pole the timely-escaped the nimble-footed hilton opens the first hotel, 88.3 BELOW ZERO, where still panting in her hastily laced corset the begum rents a south-facing suite. For a gold piece, a raging rat in her girdle, where a fig of desire was strangled.

haha hiltons here too, just look
h.h. peeling his egg and tapping an old nail
on the head
to the right: the proud owner beside his ochre-painted veteran
gadzooks, a lovely print

2.

My grandfather read marx along the railway line
from akkrum to ijlst
and I, lying against the crooked sleepers
of his twill trousers,
chewed grass and thought of old shatterhand,
pissed still awkward in his cap before the strike

a deeply devout indian, before he ate
he called on sanctus drincatibus
then straight to pray his fill with total application
his whiskers smelled of tobacco and trains

he told jokes
and died

Who left bloodrust in the snow?
the corpse of the still warm sniper
steams to his touch
it leaves him cold that near sedan
a peasant hoes up his grandfather:
brecht is a hit and gleaming auto-
mobiles stand waiting outside the theatre.
gold-braided caps smoke quick fags
behind the wheel but still respect
the chalk-line. fed to death, fattened prime beef,
                                              vaguely dreaming
of tough talk, a night of rusty knives

threnos

Light of how many suns;
and monstrous wind blows across the white-scorched plain
bone-meal and women's hair
the indistinguishable lump of flesh, blotched
in vulnerable cellars
farmers search the white weeds for an eyeball

war throttles tenochca
in the hunting-ground of the past

— when nobody saw me; I in the shadow
of diabolical machines began that flight towards the sun,
pent-up still in halfsleep, bellyful of welcome and greetings
on brochures of summery cities, sandstone ruins and statues,
and shanty-towns like a rusty ravine —

    where one dies of the expert prostitution
    of kids and old crones,
    brasilia coffee and tea and scum
    that colours the waters, rust-brown
    the water from bombay to bogotá

we had no macanas left
it rained all night
we ate worms and rats
and smelled the powder
that charred the shields

> "after the battle a great many were baptized
> and we taught them christ's law"
> at the extortionate museum north of naples
> yes, here we go again: tears freeze,
> black those butterflies of glass

war still throttles tenochca
on the volcano's membrane

> where penderecki locks his iron strings in sound-
> blocks and lamentations

farmers search the white weeds for an eyeball
in vulnerable cellars
the indistinguishable lump of blotched flesh
bone-meal and women's hair
and monstrous wind blows across the white-scorched plain.
light of how many suns

3.

> Return after the murder of mercedes, his favourite bird:
> her half-open mouth, how the grass there is still wet
>   with rain
> her moist tawny hand clutching the elder-branch
> his fish, his cross-member penetrating; and
> my birth approaches like a flood-tide

>   . . . return to the base

and stand in the hall, the growth
of this ice-tumour quickly gathers momentum

then wind, blue marble the snowbridge in southern light
and I: komachi we're alone now

she sits motionless between crates
the house with its chinks sealed up
knobs handles
snap like knives. breath on breath:
a hymn of shrinking membranes under glass, the leaf

frost falters on the leaf
nothing moves

the cold spreads soundlessly
both masked dressed for eternal winter
the ovary armoured, the locked massif
the empty seed-vessel, the frozen gesture

> The outside of the body. Where does her face begin, where does my hand end? The inside of the body. Fields of white. Drifting white ice-floes, but no encounter as time drifts between and distances people, sitting motionless, at ever greater speed. There she is now, primped, decked out on the carpet, while time sneaks off with her and space bulges like a breast.
> Does she send word? she can't. Do I send word? her eyes no longer visible as though the narrow slits are overgrown with moss to protect the iris the retina the pupil for the journey backwards.
> She is further off now.
> And I too journeying backwards. The gap between the floes widens. Slowly she's stretched on her carpet, tilted back, rushing ahead like a speck, immobile in her skin. And I too tumbling back, but hanging motionless off my hands. Space warps at the speed of light, atop her high back the body is stretched out like a nebula and curls down at the edges. I lie in belts of absence and expect to expect myself. Yes I say, yes expect me; and she, behind pinions of milky ways, rises in backward attack and

saké is best in autumn
from the jar of shojo, from the magical fountain
the saké still flows

both in butsu
a flower, Awoi!
like a flower
both, komachi and shosho

Notes:

The name Petrus Toen occurs on the back of the 15th-century Flemish diptych 'Portrait of a Man', attributed to the Master of the Ursula Legend. The portrait may represent Petrus Toen, as the name was not uncommon in Bruges at the time. In the Latin text the word 'ExTRViS' should be read as 'EXSTRVIS'. (See H. Pauwels, *De eeuw der Vlaamse Primitieven*, Bruges, 1960).

The Polish composer Krzysztof Penderecki wrote 'Threnos' (1960) for the victims of Hiroshima.

The Japanese motif at the end alludes to the Noh play *Sotoba Komachi*, in which Komachi has lost her lover Shojo because she made an impossible demand, which caused his death. Consumed by remore Komachi tries to establish contact with Shojo's spirit so as to be reunited with her lover beyond death. At the end of the play *Kayoi Komachi* the chorus observes that the two have finally come together in Buddha: "They both became pupils of Buddha, both Komachi and Shosho." (See Ezra Pound and Ernest Fenollosa, *The Classic Noh Theatre of Japan*). There are, of course, numerous variants of this motif.

"Awoi" is a fleeting reference to the court lady Awoi ("Flower of the East"), jealous lover of Genji. See Murasaki Shikibu's 11th-century novel *Genji Monogatari*, and the Noh play *Awoi no Uye* as translated by Pound and Fenollosa.

(H.C.t.B.)

from: *The White Shaman*

Maker & Model

1.

The poem an image empty
as possible of the maker
that therein coincides with the model

the pickle of names corrodes the whiteness
of what is not known
            but called up
in the train of a swift invocation

I renounce all the names
covering the void
like a nude with its better picture

I beg your pardon
for the room I fill
that I still live in a house, draw breath
use words and margarine, and
make myself scarce

word after word I put behind me
                      and so
fetch harness and pithily curb the lip
of those close penned by this earthy mews

2.

Also I put behind me   word after word
a tortuous distance;
    I read the blank
mountain chart of an empty dream   and climb

and drop

    and follow vanished paths

        towards the white-furred valley

    I describe
a spiral
    towards the white word-crystal
that is relinquished last

I hack
    and shape
a winding stair
    of missing
        treads

so that I step into my emptiness

        and fall

    where I am absent
driven into the snowy glare
        of the first beginning

I curl up
    in the lonely snail-shell
        of this universe

        the poem   an image
empty as possible of the maker
who therein coincides with the model

The white shaman: an initiation

1.

To fly in over the sound,
over dark bowls of finnish lakes

to board the kayak
of the dead

to drift on the waters
between taiga and tundra

to purge eye and ear
in expanse and emptiness

to feed on berries, with cap
and odour of the divine mushroom

to dream the dream
of the eternal present

like an arctic bear
retire once more into snowblind drunkenness

2.

In waning afternoon light
to melt seven flakes on the tongue

to stoop into the tent
as the drowsed sun sinks behind woodland

full-length on a bed of leaves
to blow the smouldering birch-bark fire

to spy through the smoke-hole
on the white-blue polestar

in limpid joy to observe the celestial nail
and shining navel of one's universe

to leave the tent on all fours
for a distant rustling of wings

eye to eye with the white wolves
of a brief dawn

The other sleep

Grey light, late swans in taut flight
    past faint contours of receding mountains

come from fergana by heavenly horse
    and now at the margin of ice-bound marshes

southward the road that divides on the autumnal plateau:
    notion of mist around nomads on horseback,

flash of a train dust-red erupting from the mountain flanks –
    and low in the western basin the yellow yolk of the sun.

brought here by guides, ill-trained but well
    equipped I sit on moss between meagre birches

poking the ashes of an age-old fireplace;
    moist nostrils, eyebrows bristling with frost

an early snow-hare detects too late the scent
    of the preying fox

Here reckoned among the idlers,
    there cold-shouldered as morose

I claim to know nothing more
    than what my hand has shaped or shapes;

left ignorant by thinking,
    in everything the beginner who unlearns

and then attempts again
    to make wet wood catch fire.

creaky, crest-fallen, nonetheless
    delving from dreams ancestral forms:

still, the hare at last roasted! but then, with a crick,
    carried tentward as a try-square

by inquisitive hunters (who'd heard it rumoured
    that the czar was murdered long ago)

That'll really be something when the revolution
    of the alienated bursts upon the city!

although recovered the body wavers
    in immense emptiness

and obscene silence fells the mind
    like a birch;

o cool womb —
    earth, even the flexible spear of the slow and

distant sun grazes your skin here like a shingle
    skimming over water,

numb through summer and winter, clinched
in the cold of ages, the earth's crust —

pierced only by what has died;
    the rustle of rats grows louder in the shrubs

Tormented, in his tent on the mound
    the stubborn straggler from the west

who sleeps only to catch up
    with sleep eventually,

who lost in sunken lives
    slowly sinks into the dark tidal forest below.

the sopping plains stiffen,
    growing frost unlocks the marsh;

fur-hunters blast him awake: dragged into
    what present? primeval booty in the bog?

(dead mammoths still carry live
    germs of splenic fever under their skin;

the meat bat-grey and rancid as mutton
    strikes eager eaters with eternal sleep)

Recall images of people,
    tough and supple as a spine:

the girl at Windeby — she with the blindfold,
    strangled in the peat and tanned

like a cow-hide between layers of oak-bark;
    the red-haired venus of Yde, smeared

with corpse-fat; the man at Grauballe — locked
    in terror, with ripped throat,

stripped of life
    like a text of significance,

but still pinned by forked stakes
    to the bottom of the bog

and then covered with osier,
    tough and supple as a spine

"in the moss-grown basin at the tree-line"

A grave; the unhurried shovelling begins,
    layer after layer slowly spaded away:

a soapstone bowl and vestiges of fire,
    we hit upon signs —

splintered language
    scratched on an oracle tooth.

then, through clefts in the petrified mud
    the velvet double-image of black eyes appears

— as of dead lovers, surprised in the act
    and never seen again by friends;

wrecked by time and accident
    but now a prey to clotted rapture —

still anticipating birth
    and preoccupied with death already

Is the raven on its way?
    is the bear not yet loose?

here, under the wide-brimmed hats
    of drovers and preachers,

firm in the saddle — the horse-fly
    crushed on the forehead,

by the road that divides,
    between receding pine and approaching plateau —

where the wood grows sparse as a poet's hair,
    on the edge of hoof-beat and heaven's fire

we part,
    damp down the sparks

and fuel dormancy to feed the waking
    mind with signs of emptiness and life

Second song of the shaman

1.

Once more the age demanded an image;

   the grass people meanwhile
in the import- and exploit-barbarians' grip
  who also pave the snotty paths
   of political depravity

no mountain, nor even a tree
breaks the sloppy morass
  where spectators and makers
   powerless because compromised
take in all the shortcomings
  that under the tight-fitting suit
  of limited ability
poor ventriloquists
  visibly conceal

that is an image

truthful but not fruitful
fruitful but not truthful
  like a weapon
  that can in the drumfire
  of perfidious wit
forever benumb
  the song's vigour

2.

There's plenty of snivelling
for the goddes;
        her poetic nest odour
is full of promise
yet a perfect match for the lie

it is therefore advisable
to say still more in still
less words

so to steer the hand
that ear and eye
        incessantly move
   in space and white stillness
        between the lines

to cherish thought
but always with a feel
for the act

to test the voice
for its timbre and tone,
    the tongue
with dwarflike determination
restrained —

        yet with invariable recalcitrance
     clamouring like hell
whenever at breakneck speed
   verbal violence
       threatens to gain ground

3.

I think most artfully
    in poetry
        not in some forced palaver

so I make
    and soon
        a mask of grass

        creep incognito
past sleek lawns of wit
and shady fabrications

        slip unseen
from summer salting and light slumber
into the unshorn reed-bed of sleep

        and imagine there:
the opened poem
        that does not confirm
what is manifest,
        but sets free
what locked in itself
has found its form again just now

Doorpost of a Tsimshian house, Kitwancool, British Columbia.
Photograph H. C. ten Berge, 1975.

from: *Va-banque*

Tongue tied

I

Whatever is uttered
    or swallowed
has spent the night with the shaded organ
which behind firm or false teeth
lives its fleshy life in halflight

having learnt
to speak
it gradually entrenches itself in speech

the mouth lends words
    the dazzle-paint of simplicity
which in turn
    in a manner of speaking
grants poetry its shape

II

Poetry is said to exist
when it sets the tongue wagging

it thrives on rumour
being passed on by word of mouth

the tongue that penetrates language
    down to its most sensitive membrane
drives the line
instantly
    into ecstatic intercourse

III

A fish in the sluice
between inside and out

a snail without a shell, asleep
under the mouth's bare roof

a hamster storing verbal seed
in each cheek-pouch

IV

The mouth opens like a golden box,
the tongue swims around, emitting words
at intervals

love and poetry
are forever on the tip of one's tongue

what began as a chemical reaction
between brain and bum
finds its shape
when pushed into expression

love and poetry
are therefore on the tip of one's tongue

the mouth opens like a golden box,
the tongue swims around, emitting words
at intervals

V. 1

A slave, a scourge, a snotfish
in the half-aquatic realm
of membranes, spittle, slime
behind coated palisades

tossing restlessly at each passage
between darkness and light
or slumbering on a breath of air
each time it brushes past

V. 2

Although tickled by food
he shows himself piqued

he reveals
what is covered up
and lashes
whatever offends him

he loosens tongues
              yet remains shackled
to the clearing-house
where everything feels clammy
              and powerless
he stoops to kiss the green backs of teeth

V. 3

I take the mouth's compliance
so much for granted
that I forget the slave
who feeds my thoughts

sentenced
to lifelong lip-service
he becomes the fettered master
of my mouth

when I talk while I eat
he senses how bread and speech
love each other in his den

he eagerly worms
his way in —
nimble piglet, snugly
wallowing in the pulp

But no tongue can muzzle love for long

when the phrase is ready and the bread
undressed, he lets the word-lump
out and gobbles up the rest

VI

No longer a mirage of the senses but an image
of the essence

The Lusitanian variant

I

Fortunes in knickerbockers
walk the familiar paths
    of political roulette

it was karlsbad then,
now estoril beyond sintra (sterile &
                  smooth as a shaven abdomen)

to the right stands the bank of the holy ghost &
                  commerce,
to the left a dark-skinned minion
empties the casino's tiled cesspit

itinerant carpet-vendors
squirt phlegm into fish-baskets

sweat bites into cracked lips,
toy windmills whirring in the breeze

today's possessors
are tomorrow's possessed

The eye wanders
    past palm-trees and flower-beds,
  lingers
at the ornamental waters, the iceman, the pickpocket,
                the dozing donkey-rider

over there, behind rambling rose and bear's breech
the shimmering straw hats of
stiff gentlemen   who tremulous
    and blue
predict a certain future for the past

II

    In my skin
in my chair   in my garden
    I sip my iced tea

declare my abhorrence
    of rebels

hasten to flatter fugitive sovereigns
with hopes of a golden
    herebefore
and stake myself
as the plaything of thriftless
            oil-barons

I exhort the humane but dread the god-fearing,
stray with the straying, swear with the sworn —

I swallow a pill against retching

and in the gaming-rooms
hob-nob with powdered mothers

I'm available as
steward, bedfellow, if required
even as tutor
        to their degenerate litter

In the quiet hours
I steer my cabriolet
to the quinta,
        and mount a make-
believe daughter in a hot bean-field

III. 1 Duel

We go on a tour of duty
along forgotten roads

I play on the mind
and dwell in the heart
      of a high-ranking commander

I'm the rebel
he invariably subdues

we're as reined in as we're unbridled

when I play him off
he holds me back

what divides us
also unites us

we decide to join
forces

O mystique of the first beginning

already the little spark of the soul
leaps across

he has it my way
and I take control
      of his thoughts

III. 2 Place of reckoning

A dwarf-chapel full of pig's ears

surrounded
by crutches and chaste madonnas,
petrified tumours and artificial
joints, animal masks and
faded in memoriam cards from a previous reign of terror

intoxicated
by antiseptic gauze and litanies, urine,
bottled lymph and rosaries
that unequivocally and
irrefutably demonstrate the miraculous
healing of fatally afflicted parts of
body and nation alike

we finally, around three o'clock,
in that dark dantesque place,
before the holy trinity
of gold, goods and god
(in the latter's house)
in our own interest and the nation's
plot and conspire

III. 3 Euphoria

Mafra: a dream-
        palace turned into a barracks,
the lusitanian escorial
        a cold grave

walls and stables already covered
in graffiti
                CONTRA A MISÉRIA!

The sun-glasses off and into
the lofts

the future, I say, must not see
suffering like this

a haze of words, an extra ration of rum
has transported the militia
into a state of rapture

the troops climb onto the tables

I pronounce
in certain terms
against the present
        and expound
what I don't understand myself

today's possession-takers
are tomorrow's dispossessed

Ringed by laughing squaddies
I let myself be caught
in a snapshot

"the captain shares bread and wine
with the men"

— the mug is passed round, the brain
abuzz with rumour

the wenches go flaunting fruit-
fully in the streets,
heavy-breasted
mothers are hawking over-
ripe apples

in the mountains the donkeys groan
under women in widow's weeds

III. 4 Dança mortal

I'd wanted to go hunting
partridges before nightfall

the village square quivers forlornly in the sun

Where I used to play in the old days
I'm pie-eyed on the hoof

An ambush: suddenly
enclosed by a hedge of high-pitched voices

I stand transfixed in a field —

instantly
disarmed by children

The dip goes round in a song
and helplessly I'm counted out:

> *One's for your dress made of water*
> *Two's for your body of bread*
> *Three's for I'll eat up your daughter*
> *Four's for your hands are all red*
>
> *One to four and who cares?*
> *Better say your prayers*
> *'Cause now you're dead!*

The heat soils the body,
afternoon turns to lead on the skin

flies are coppering the eye-sockets
of a carcass

it's later than I thought:

I'd wanted to go hunting
partridges before nightfall

III. 5 Russian roulette

First we'd had a drop to drink
under the cork-tree

then we'd gone on boozing
leaning against the pines

I got depressed, he
rowdy

we drifted down
towards the olives

and killed the night
with cards and bottles

in the end we had nothing left
to say

a fire-eater sat roasting
jugged hare

Round about six I decided to place the explosives
under the house of the holy ghost &
                                        commerce —

the porter left
and no-one took his place;

we put on livery
and take turns to guard the glass

whoever's marked down
will be blown to bits with the rest

IV *Praia des maçãs*

A high coast in a haze of sleep

languid drifters
traverse the sun and the sea-green
dream of lost americas

a reef sprays light behind the breakers

wine on the western slopes,
paths bordered with agaves
and arid fields burnt in the valley

steep reeds crouching by the springs

sunlight smoulders
round about the hills
in dismantled forts and convents

the game was over here
before it was ever begun

    A white moon ripens
early above the fields,
the salt wind renews its grip on the skin

> *goddess on the cactus*
> *goddess in the sand,*
> *the stalk of the maize*
>   *is growing in your hand!*

women and crows start up
at the window

start up
and regroup

a voice carves
a song in the twilight —

goddess on the cactus
goddess in the sand,
my tongue
    steals the salt from your lips
my mouth
    drinks the dew from your hand;

child, you know what I want
I ask for no caresses,
when the wind goes through the maize
it ruffles both your tresses!

The heart is slow and impetuous

a spring-tide of seed breaks
in the core
of wet caves

the high coast in a haze of sleep

but the sea

    down

        there,

the sea

    down

        there

            drunkenly combs the apple-beach

NEMRUD DAGH

Wrokkend als bejaarde stieren staan de bergen

Tot de westelijke Eufraat

Droogte kerft en tekent wegen vol inskripties.

Ik lift mee vanaf de basis. Denk: mâsjallâh,

Wat een meisje! Na een uur lopen we

Vast in Commagene waar Antiochus de Anatoliër

Een breed terras met goden dreef

Geen karrespoor en geen kameel, we steken

In de nesten. Haar keel een rasp

Die gramschap spuit; ik slik

Gestoken woorden in en fluit

Een jagersdeun onder de motorkap. De zon schijnt

(Schijnt) zonder duur verhaast ondraaglijke

Sur place boven een bergrug in het westen

~~Ze zijn nog anders van gezien gebroken~~
(zijn nog ongebroken)

Ze wijst op het terras waar vogels

Zijn versteend; een aangevreten beeld

Tuurt in de spleten van de aarde

Koppen staan verspreid, gepaquelleerd

Tussen de keien;

Starend naar de ~~Weken~~ die ...

[Breuklijn] grond raakt (plotseling) in beweging

Heuvels kantelen naderbij
De aarde schrokt haar goden op

En trekt een ring van ogen om ons heen

Het kijken enz.

Nemrud Dagh – revised version (by courtesy of H.C. ten Berge) from: *New Poems*

The Hartlaub gull

For B.B. who is doing nine years in the cooler

    A dream vision, Breyten, the print
    of the bay
        you were mailing
    as I went up in smoke
      of pipe tobacco and jet engines
        over
            the empty sea —

the table full of maps and dates
no shelter, no sunshield,
      wine in the shadow
        of dusty shrubs;
colour haze behind us — all
so distant
    that the island kept escaping the lens.

There and then are now
preserved;
    eternal present
is an image projected on the wall:

on the left a killer, hat
      over gutted eyes,
on the right a pimp
      with the sidelong glance of a vagrant

your one hand is caught
    in flight above the table top
the other meets out of shot
    with soft resistance of
        a neck or thigh or ovenwarm lap —

silently, attentively
we are on show

(is that the blur of the beloved's
hair fanning the edge?)

Boland close by and the jug
        far off as yet
we saw a white ant
run from Windhoek to Verneukpan
where a sweet fruit
        was baked to a mummy by the sun.

Back then that man on the beach
with a gull on his head,
a monkey fled from your sketchpad;
        the wind
carried the fragrance
of women and bird dung, seaweed and tar —

Yet,
like Cook on his voyages
I see that island again,
        a place,
where it is better to be a gull
than a human being

James C
(27.IV.1775)
> As we sailed from Table Bay we observed *Robben Island*, a barren, sandy place where many murderers and other felons are held prisoner by the Dutch East India Company, though there are also some poor unfortunates among them, victims of the merciless ambition of these same merchants, such as the King of *Madura* who, robbed of his possessions and driven to the utmost despair, lives the hard miserable life of a common slave there.

Certainly, a sandy
place, where two centuries
later another visitor
slightly shifted the point of view

Most of all (he writes) I enjoyed
a camp on Robben Island in Table Bay
The island — no larger than Sark —
is inhabited by a small military garrison

Due to the great hospitality and assistance
of the commander, Major Anderson,
we could camp
undisturbed
a few hundred yards from the gull colony

We were primarily interested
in the aggressive behaviour
these animals showed
when defending their territory
against their neighbours

The ten days on Robben Island flew by —
and so there was little time for more
than this cursory survey

Nevertheless
(Nico T adds)
nevertheless
we were not dissatisfied.

Says the Vagrant
who blows neither hot nor cold,

    — another bullshit artist I suppose,
a versifier measuring by two standards
in the land of Cockaigne;

while I'm pimping I'll take
        no smooth talker,
so whoever, at this place, here,
passes the apposite fart
gets one square on the mouth, gratis and for free.

The travesty, my friend, after the tragedy.

Intra Muros

For yolande and the lotus eater

In the rue de Vaugirard
there's a message on a wall

Lotus: changez votre décor

I'll gladly take it to heart
now I'm walking beside her delicate smile
and near the same wall where I
buy pumpkins the street has
suddenly altered

Adjusted sonnet

A wall and a wall and a wall and a wall with a door
a sketch of a wall and a wall and a wall and a wall with a door
a coat and a shoe and a lemon and a pad on a table
a sketch of a coat and a shoe and a lemon and a pad on a table
a letter and a hand and a mouth and a midge
a sketch of a letter and a hand and a mouth and a midge
an eye and a mouth and a shoe and a wall
a sketch of an eye and a mouth and a shoe and a wall
a lemon and a coat and a letter and a wall
a sketch of a lemon and a coat and a letter and a wall
a shoe and a hand and an eye and a wall with a door
a sketch of a shoe in a hand and an eye in a wall with no door
are real are real repeat I repeat I stress are after all
real signs of life outside four fireproof seamless walls

How many months since you went
— "on to Wellington with long strides" —
and exchanged nostalgia for the boarding-house
with cellars
where the fathers are tuning automatic violins
and the cream of cape voices
are singing psalms *a cappella*

rooms betrayed the reek of cuban cigars
microphones sucked the words out of your skin

from between sheets and flowers
indifferent glass eyes kept a look-out for you

who was it massaged a lullaby
into your ears, what inconspicuous fairy
connived with the dark
that suddenly swallowed you —

Ill-fitting poem

Behind pupil-painted spectacles
workaday deeds are worked out

"how with one mind they league together"

warm hands, cold heart
folk know themselves on sundays in god's house
fresh-clad and whitewashed;
boor bones propping bottle, bible
and wenched to their one and only very own

"strike down the might of the backsliding rebel"

better run to the bad
than sneak back halfway

you're stuck where you are
and remember the dust
filmed eyes of egyptian camels

Ill-adjusted sonnet

Even as I read
how this country's underworld of hacks
keeps on its feet
with frenetic trifles,
poetry hides as it always does
in abandoned rooms, in your bare cell

twilight and water as far as the winter-dyke
a girl comes by on a white horse

after four years filled with silence
the mail brings greetings
from prison
and we sit around the table
still
celebrating a reunion

25.1.80/4.30 p.m.

There is a question you don't raise
and finally ask anyway —
             how we manage to retain and control
our ability to arrange,
to model and to mould,
in the teeth of the omnipotent presence of the racketeers

"Roll on time (you write)
I'd like to be buying wine and dates again

you know what I'm hoping for?"

take my thick skin coat, Breyten,
now you winter in the tropics for so long

The path of seclusion too
leads to revolt,
like a russian peasant you stand
on moss-cold stones

from: *Texan Elegies*

A semblance of reality

Winter was as always
Cold
Hats and coats
Turned all the fathers in the picture
Old

You were nowhere, hardly
A tippler in the nocturnal sea

For heart's-blood and hate came
In scanty measures then
            said the man
Who was unwittingly to father you

He worked for a mouthful of stale bread
A gentleman,
    so had nothing
To say

You see pursed lips and a kingsize
Nose under an undersized hat

Caries even then
Fretted his teeth and his legs
Were sheathed in longjohns

My dreams burnt out
My wife too chaste by half
I grew timid on the road
And shy in my own house
    he wrote in ink along the margins

That uncertain laugh
That flapping of his hands

Look at the flaxen hair
About his ear, the duffel
Coat buttons, the ash-cone
Of his cigar

(A brother to be approaches
Unmoved)

The image is slightly
Snowy,
      eyes
Half-closed

All those years flakes fell around the sleigh
With which we'd later leave a track
At full trot through untrodden fields

He stands alone with his laugh
And for an instant
Comes close to himself

To be alive was an infliction

It might, said father,
Have been a lot worse

Switching off then
And there

We agree: all this is past
Reality
        shrunk
To a snapshot three by four

You know this is not living
But a dead
Instant discreetly written
Back to life

What was is now
Only in spirit
And what the spirit is
Heaven knows

As you too start to shrivel, fragment
And crumble
        you make the most
Of pictured snippets of a bygone time

All proved to be finite: the country lane,
The father, a love
And all changed under your hands

Vivacious cells renewed themselves
The earth stayed silent as the grave

Old men were in time to prevent
A threatened peace
But you soldiered on

They prized your head, were out to win
Your heart
        but you took to your heels

Steering clear of incense
And the noose; knife-prick
Pepper, atrocities on paper
Were alien to you

As if unrequited loves no longer mattered
You avoided company
And suffered sores under the skin

Tissues were imperturbably
Built up and eaten away

The inaccessible girlfriend remained inaccessible

Only in your dream
 as snow began falling slowly
She slept on the narrow bed in the house
At the edge of the wood
Where you timidly fondled her breasts once
And the room glowed with innocence

You read the Great Well-Spring of Love
And saw Wendelmoet Claesdochter
 of Ilpendam in her

"Happy is the comb
 of gilded ivory
That plies these tresses . . ."

She became a name on a door, a quivering
Of nostrils in a chock-full bar,
One moment she stood in high boots of light
 behind a window

At times you smelled her scent in another's coat
You travelled to the city in vain, popped
Up in the remotest corners, scanned
The personal columns in all the dailies

Now and then there was music, or
A voice through a wall
Speaking a distant emotion

Years later in the house where your father died
You found among newspaper clippings, wartime

Scrip and snapshots of fuddled
      wedding guests
That forgotten note
      written in ink
In her girlish hand

"We shall meet each other
In the dark filled with shame
Secretly weeping among clutter rusting
In the rye field"

You knew that was not living
But a dead
Instant of someone breathless
With love who still lived on

Who secretly now
    media vita
Recalls the solace of her sobbing
Like a lucid dream seen but not seen through

Death sits on a branch; a father
    rakes the garden with a practised hand

And sullenly asks
    what all those words might mean

There is no picture, so
    it looks like a frame-up

You dig a heel
    into half-rotten leaves

A hectic flush
    covers you skull to neck

Thrushes are scuffling in the privet
    doing a silent deal with the worms

A mother comes by
    bashfully on her way to church

You mutter something about imagination
    the fruits of the spirit

What you invoke
    was never there

His rake smites the earth
    between the roses

Hands form mudras in the air
    eyes are two wasp-stings

He makes to speak, picks
    and weighs every word

Like a shrew that licks its lips
    under an undersized hat

That yonder, he says with a wave of his arm
    towards the house of prayer on the green

That yonder fooled me all my life
    with the fruits of the spirit

He laughs a thin, high laugh
    and stands alone among the roses

from: *Songs of Anguish and Despair*

Nothing to begin with, nothing
at the end

between beginning and end
(in between)

it buds, it lifts
its head

Once it leaves the ground
it can only be guessed at

like a flower never seen
blown in from wild gardens

suddenly glowing,
sowing in our eyes

(while the unknown
ripens and scatters its seed)

as many times over
ecstatic light

that leaves us then
just as suddenly emptied

30.06.86

Whoever dies in the poem
is raised at a stroke of the pen

"the dead baker pushes a bread-cart
rattling over the cobbles"

This is no dream, this is
an exemplary sentence

doing its job, prepared if need be
to stop dead or continue

into this or that street
where girls in white bonnets once

scrubbed the porches and a servant
whistled a popular tune

where they danced and fell foul, ate
salt herring or put

their soul into love's
old sweet song

while a stranger turns
a corner lost in thought —

a passing prophet perhaps, displaced
priest, clown, god knows

maybe a child molester or heavenly
courier in a mackintosh

who now slows down
addresses the baker, inhales

the smell of bread and sweat
buys the one remaining tart

and asks him the way to the hereafter

A.

I minimolens: bestaan in het nederlands evenmin. Analogie: minirok / minishirt.
waarom die verklarende vertaling?
Molentjes bij overigens een ontbrekend plastic tegenwoordig ↔ snorrend geluid.

II de godvruchtigen: etymologische woordspeling niet bewust. Gewoon: vrome kwezels met wie je moet oppassen; hebben ze achter de elleboog als puntje bij paaltje komt. Doe wat je goed dunkt.

worg: 'benauwdheid in de keel, stikkend gevoel". "Quinsy" is toch meer een ziekte (angina)! "worg" is zo'n heerlijk, bijna fysiek 'stikkend'-woord; een beetje goor en gluiperig ook, precies wat bij deze figuren past. Heeft "quinsy" die gevoelswaarde ook?
Worg is i.c. ook: bijna stikken van jezelf en niet voorzorg een pil slikken

aanpappen: "rub shoulders" even sterk als eventuele varianten? (suck up to).
In 'gamblers' kringen is de sucker trouwens een bekende verschijning.

desnoods: mag door desgewenst (if desired) vervangen worden indien de engelse versie daardoor versterkt zou worden. Creative translation is niet principieel onverwerpelijk.

worp: hier ook grof bedoeld. "Off-spring" is veel te netjes. Gebruik gerust de dierlijke betekenis.

III. 2 Titel: moeilijk te beoordelen door mij. Zoenplaats ook verzoenplaats; verzoeningsplaats; waar zoenoffers worden gebracht en de zonen zwenders en sed ewersen en zich verzoenen.

diminutive: vgl. minimolens. Ook dwergkapel is ongebruikelijk in het nederlands; waarom dan niet in het engels? Er gaat sowieso veel verloren door zo'n lang adjectief dat weinig pregnant is. (Cf: dwergberk = dwarfbirch.)

III. 3 "~~[illegible]~~ (~~[illegible]~~) ~~[illegible]~~ ~~[illegible]~~" (~~[illegible]~~ ~~[illegible]~~)

... wordt niet /meer geleden: een valkuil doordat 'meer' op de volgende regel staat. → ① Er zal niet meer worden geleden / ② Er zal niet méér worden geleden (dan nu al het geval is);
dus zal er iets moeten komen in deze trant: There will be no more suffering (of iets dergelijks)

"In the future no
more suffering, I say"

de gevoelige plant:, hier is bewust een ouderwetse, zo niet onbollige uitdrukking gebruikt. Hopelijk is er ~~gevoel~~ in de engelse versie iets dergelijks aan de hand: kan dit niet beoordelen.

de voorlaatste strofe: ik besef dat deze moordend is om te vertalen. Er zou een geheel nieuwe engelse versie moeten geschreven worden, in eendrachtige samenwerking eventueel. D.w.z. het nederlands grotendeels los laten en tot een creatieve omzetting zien te komen, want:
- "girls" is juist iets te netjes ('t zijn volksmeiden) → zij gaan achter de binken aan!
- de relatie binken - venten is onovertdraagbaar, etc. Ik geef het al toe: Inderdaad, (enigszins) hopeloos! Toch gloort er enig licht, hoop ik, wanneer je vrijheden durft nemen en Paul Vincent enigermate vertrouwd is met engelse taalgebruiken die "op de rand" of juist daarover zijn. Laat eens weten hoe dit afloopt. Ben graag tot hulp bereid.

Comments by the author on the early version of 'The Lusitanian Variant', 1979.

from: *Rites of Passage*

River landscape with blue bottle

I

An azure streak on white fields;
Veined ice, glass pierced by light

River landscape with bottle

Its open mouth a blue emptiness
caressed by space

Its base planted in earth,
It cranes up at the stars

II

The empty bottle goggles into space,
Low skyline severs its neck

The spirit has flown,
the wind drags

Bone-marrow frosted on the tofts

Cold ices the lymph
In the inflamed eye of the sun

III

Here black water
There dark ice

Thin-filmed, blow-holed, last birds' refuge

Blue splash on white fields,
Heart shrivelling under sky-grey

A leveret dies on the plain,
A marten dashes through apple-trees

IV

Frost-smoke above stubble;
Birch contours, ice-moored, in drowned land

Crouched behind dykes
Broken roofs groan under a low sky

Brown reed, corn buntings cheeping on the stakes

A buzzard crops the dead hare;
A shotgun cracks on the bank

V

Wedge of grey geese in flight;
A wild duck brought down over water

Snow levels the fens at last

The bottle, its blue neck bared.
Wind and light embrace it

Sound is sealed; the open mouth traps a crystal
That settles at the base

*Another Dutch Title
From Forest Books*

A Vanishing Emptiness

*Selected Poems of
Willem M. Roggeman*

Edited by Yann Lovelock

Illustrated by the Belgian pop artist Pol Mara

Willem M. Roggeman has been called a Flemish painter with words. There is no rhetoric in his work, but a balance of verbal colours, short dabs that build up to a general impression, and sentences deployed with the rhythm of brush strokes. The image leaps from the page.

ISBN 0 948259 51 5   paper £7.95   96pp illustrated